'I hate and
And if you ask
me how, I do not
know: I only feel
it, and I'm torn
in two.'

ERLESTOKE
LIBRARY

GAIUS VALERIUS CATULLUS
Born *c.* 84 BCE
Died *c.* 54 BCE

Taken from Peter Whigham's translation of *The Poems*,
first published in 1966.

CATULLUS IN PENGUIN CLASSICS
The Poems

CATULLUS

I Hate and I Love

Translated by
Peter Whigham

PENGUIN BOOKS

PENGUIN CLASSICS

UK | USA | Canada | Ireland | Australia
India | New Zealand | South Africa

Penguin Books is part of the Penguin Random House group of companies
whose addresses can be found at global.penguinrandomhouse.com.

This selection published in Penguin Classics 2015
002

Translation copyright © Peter Whigham, 1966

The moral right of the translator has been asserted

Set in 9/12.4 pt Baskerville 10 Pro
Typeset by Jouve (UK), Milton Keynes
Printed in Great Britain by Clays Ltd, St Ives plc

A CIP catalogue record for this book is available from the British Library

ISBN: 978-0-141-39859-4

www.greenpenguin.co.uk

MIX
Paper from
responsible sources
FSC® C018179
www.fsc.org

Penguin Random House is committed to a
sustainable future for our business, our readers
and our planet. This book is made from Forest
Stewardship Council® certified paper.

1

To whom should I present this
little book so carefully polished
but to you, Cornelius, who have always
been so tolerant of my verses,

                        you
who of us all has dared
to take the whole of human history
as his field

        – three doctoral and weighty volumes!
Accept my book, then, Cornelius
for what it's worth,

        and may the Muse herself
turn as tolerant an eye upon these songs

        in days to come.

5

Lesbia
     live with me
& love me so
we'll laugh at all
the sour-faced strict-
ures of the wise.
This sun once set
will rise again,
when our sun sets
follows night &
an endless sleep.
Kiss me now a
thousand times &
now a hundred
more & then a
hundred & a
thousand more again
till with so many
hundred thousand
kisses you & I
shall both lose count
nor any can
from envy of
so much of kissing
put his finger
on the number

of sweet kisses
you of me &
I of you,
darling, have had.

6

Your most recent acquisition, Flavius,
must be as unattractive as
                    (doubtless) she is unacceptable
or you would surely have told us about her.
You are wrapped up with a whore to end all whores
and ashamed to confess it.
                    You do not spend bachelor nights.
Your divan, reeking of Syrian unguents,
draped with bouquets & blossoms etc.
                              proclaims it,
the pillows & bedclothes indented in several places,
a ceaseless jolting & straining of the framework
the shaky accompaniment to your sex parade.
Without more discretion your silence is pointless.
Attenuated thighs betray your preoccupation.
Whoever, whatever she is, good or bad,
                              tell us, my friend –
Catullus will lift the two of you & your love-acts into the
    heavens
in the happiest of his hendecasyllables.

7

Curious to learn
how many kiss-
es of your lips
might satisfy
my lust for you,
Lesbia, know
as many as
are grains of sand
between the oracle
of sweltering Jove
at Ammon &
the tomb of old
Battiades the First,
in Libya
where the silphium grows;
alternatively,
as many as
the sky has stars
at night shining
in quiet upon
the furtive loves
of mortal men,
as many kiss-
es of your lips
as these might slake
your own obsessed
Catullus, dear,

Catullus

so many that
no prying eye
can keep the count
nor spiteful tongue fix
their total in
a fatal formula.

8

Break off
> fallen Catullus
>> time to cut losses,

bright days shone once,
> you followed a girl
>> here & there

loved as no other
> perhaps
>> shall be loved,

then was the time
> of love's *insouciance*,
>> your lust as her will

matching.
> Bright days shone
>> on both of you.

Now,
> a woman is unwilling.
>> Follow suit

weak as you are
> no chasing of mirages
>> no fallen love,

a clean break
> hard against the past.
>> Not again, Lesbia.

No more.
> Catullus is clear.
>> He won't miss you.

He won't crave it.
　　　　It is cold.
　　　　　　　　But you will whine.
You are ruined.
　　　　What will your life be?
　　　　　　　　Who will 'visit' your room?
Who uncover that beauty?
　　　　Whom will you love?
　　　　　　　　Whose girl will you be?
Whom kiss?
　　　　Whose lips bite?
　　　　　　　　Enough. Break.
Catullus.
　　　　Against the past.

9

Veraniolus,
first of friends,
have you returned
to your own roof
your close brothers
& your mother
still alive? In-
deed it's true you're
back again &
safe & sound
among us all.
So now I'll watch
& listen to your
anecdotes of
Spanish men &
Spanish places
told as only
you can tell them.
I shall embrace
your neck & kiss
you on the mouth
& on the eyes,
Veraniolus . . .

Of all light-hearted
men & women
none is lighter-
hearted than Cat-
ullus is to-day.

Furius, Aurelius, friends of my youth,
whether I land up in the Far East,
where the long-drawn roll of the Indian Ocean
        thumps on the beach,
or whether I find myself surrounded by Hyrcanians,
the supple Arabs, Sacians, Parthian bowmen,
or in the land where the seven-tongued Nile
        colours the Middle Sea,
whether I scale the pinnacles of the Alps
viewing the monuments of Caesar triumphant,
the Rhine, the outlandish seas of
        the ultimate Britons,
whatever Fate has in store for me,
equally ready for anything,
I send Lesbia this valediction,
        succinctly discourteous:
live with your three hundred lovers,
open your legs to them all (simultaneously)
lovelessly dragging the guts out of each of them
        each time you do it,
blind to the love that I had for you
once, and that you, tart, wantonly crushed
as the passing plough-blade slashes the flower
        at the field's edge.

13

I shall expect
you in to dine
a few days hence
Fabullus mine,
and we'll eat well
enough, my friend,
if you provide
the food & wine
& the girl, too,
pretty & willing.
I, Catullus,
promise you
wine & wit &
all the laughter
of the table
should you provide
whatever food
or wine you're able.
For, charmed Fabullus,
your old friend's purse
is empty now
of all but cobwebs!

In return, the
distillation
of Love's essence
take from me, or

whatever's more
attractive or
seductive than
Love's essence. For
Venus & her
Cupids gave my
girl an unguent,
this I'll give to
you, Fabullus, and
when you've smelt it
all you'll want the
gods to do is
make you one
gigantic nose
to smell it, always, with.

If, my irrepressible Calvus, I didn't
happen to love you more than my eyes
this hoax gift of yours would have made me
as cross as Vatinius . . .

   What have I done to deserve
such (& so many) poets?

    I am utterly demoralised.
May the gods scowl on whoever
sent you this clutch of offenders
in the first place.

   – A grateful client?
I smell Sulla, the pedagogue.
A *recherché* & freshly culled volume,
such as this, could well come from his hands.
And that's as it should be – a meet &
acceptable sign that your efforts
(on his behalf) are not wasted.
But the collection itself is implacably bad.
And you, naturally, sent it along to Catullus
– your Saturnalian *bonne-bouche* –
so that Gaius, on this of all days,
might suffer the refinements of tedium.
No. Little Calvus. You won't run away
with this – for tomorrow, when the shops open,
I shall comb the bookstalls for Caesius, Aquinus,
Suffenus – all who excel in unpleasantness –

and compound your present with interest.
Until then, hence from my home, hence
by the ill-footed porter who brought you.
Parasites of our generation. Poets I blush for.

32

Call me to you
at siesta
we'll make love
my gold & jewels
my treasure trove
my sweet Ipsíthilla,
when you invite
me lock no doors
nor change your mind
& step outside
but stay at home
& in your room
prepare yourself
to come nine times
straight off together,
in fact if you
should want it now
I'll come at once
for lolling on
the sofa here
with jutting cock
and stuffed with food
I'm ripe for stuffing
                              you,
my sweet Ipsíthilla.

34

Moving in her radiant care
chaste men and girls moving
wholly in Diana's care
     hymn her in this.

Latona's daughter, greatest
of the Olympian race, dropped
at birth beneath the olive trees
     on Delian hills,

alive over mountain passes,
over green glades and
sequestered glens,
     – in the talkative burn,

Juno Lucina in the groans
of parturition, Hecat, fear-
ful at crossed ways, the nymph
     of false moonlight.

You whose menstrual course
divides our year, stuff
the farmer's harvest barn
     with harvesting.

Sacred, by whatever name invoked
in whatever phase you wear, turn
upon our Roman brood, of old
     your shielding look.

37

Nine posts, five doors, up the Clivus
        Victoriae, stands an
unsavoury resort . . . unsavoury
        habitués inside,
who think that only they have cocks,
        that only they can ruffle
a pudendum, the rest of us
        as apt as goats. I could
cheerfully bugger you all while
        you wait, kicking your heels.
Your numbers, a hundred or so,
        leave me undaunted. Think
of the man-power involved! And
        think of me now, scribbling
each of your names in black letters
        on the house-front. For she
whom once I loved as no other
        girl has been loved lives here.
Who has fled from my touch & sight.
        Whom I fought for & could
not keep . . . A mixed bunch – successful,
        respectable men swap
places with dregs from the back-streets.
        She is open to all.
And one, who outdoes his home-grown
        rabbits – Egnatius,

the Spaniard with the beard, known for
       his wild dundrearies &
glistening teeth, assiduously
       (with native urine) scrubbed.

38

Angst,
　　　ennui & angst
consume my days & weeks,
and you have not written
or done anything to soothe my illness.
I am piqued.
　　　So much for our friendship.
Ah! Cornificius,
　　　a word from you would cure everything,
though more full of tears
　　　than a line from Simonides.

39

Because he has bright white teeth, Eg-
        natius whips out a
tooth-flash on all possible
        (& impossible) occasions.
You're in court. Counsel for defence
        concludes a moving per-
oration. (Grin.) At a funeral,
        on all sides heart-broken
mothers weep for only sons. (Grin.)
        Where, when, whatever the
place or time – grin. It could be a
        sort of 'tic'. If so, it's
a very *vulgar* tic, Egnatius,
        & one to be rid of.
A Roman, a Tiburtine or
        Sabine, washes his teeth.
Well-fed Umbrians & over-
        fed Etruscans wash theirs
daily. The dark Lanuvians
        (who don't need to), & we
Veronese, all wash our teeth . . .
        But we keep them tucked in.
We spare ourselves the nadir of
        inanity – inane
laughter. You come from Spain. Spaniards
        use their morning urine

Catullus

    for tooth-wash. To us that blinding
            mouthful means one thing &
  one only – the quantity of
            urine you have swallowed.

40

Whatever could have possessed you
to impale yourself on my iambics?
What ill-disposed deity inveigled you
Ravidus, into this one-sided contest?
Was it a letch for celebrity,
at no matter what cost?
                    – then you shall have it:
'Ravidus, loving in the place Catullus loves,
is lastingly nailed in this lampoon.'

43

O elegant whore!
>   with the remarkably long nose
unshapely feet
>   lack lustre eyes
fat fingers
>   wet mouth
and language not of the choicest,
you are I believe the mistress
of the hell-rake Formianus.

And the Province calls you beautiful;
they set you up beside my Lesbia.
O generation witless and uncouth!

45

Phyllis Corydon clutched to him
her head at rest beneath his chin.
He said, 'If I don't love you more
than ever maid was loved before
I shall (if this the years not prove)
in Afric or the Indian grove
some green-eyed lion serve for food.'

> *Amor, to show that he was pleased,*
> *approvingly (in silence) sneezed.*

Then Phyllis slightly raised her head
(her lips were full & wet & red)
to kiss the sweet eyes full of her:
'Corydon mine, with me prefer
always to serve unique Amor:
my softer flesh the fire licks
more greedily and deeper sticks.'

> *Amor, to show that he was pleased,*
> *approvingly (in silence) sneezed.*

So loving & loved so, they rove
between twin auspices of Love.
Corydon sets in his eye-lust
Phyllis before all other dust;
Phyllis on Corydon expends
her nubile toys, Love's dividends.
Could Venus yield more love-delight
than here she grants in Love's requite?

46

Now spring bursts
      with warm airs
now the *furor* of March skies
      retreats under Zephyrus . . .
and Catullus will forsake
      these Phrygian fields
the sun-drenched farm-lands of Nicaea
& make for the resorts of Asia Minor,
      the famous cities.
Now, the trepidation of departure
      now lust of travel,
feet impatiently urging him to be gone.
Good friends, good-bye,
      we, met in this distant place,
far from our Italy
      who by divergent paths
must find our separate ways home.

48

Iuventius,
were I allowed
to kiss your eyes
as sweet as honey
on & on, three
thousand kisses
would not seem
too much for me,
as many as
ripe harvest ears
of sheaves of corn
would still not be
too much of kiss-
ing you, for me.

50

The other day we spent,
Calvus, at a loose end
flexing our poetics.
Delectable twin poets,
swapping verses, testing
form & cadence, fishing
for images in wine
& wit. I left you late,
came home still burning with
your brilliance, your invention.
Restless, I could not eat,
nor think of sleep. Under
my eyelids you appeared
& talked. I twitched, feverishly,
looked for morning . . . at last,
debilitated, limbs
awry across the bed
I made this poem of
my ardour & for our
gaiety, Calvus . . . Don't
look peremptory, or
contemn my apple. Think.
The Goddess is ill-bred
exacts her hubris-meed:
lure not her venom.

51

Godlike the man who
sits at her side, who
watches and catches
    that laughter
which (softly) tears me
to tatters: nothing is
left of me, each time
    I see her,
. . . tongue numbed; arms, legs
melting, on fire; drum
drumming in ears; head-
    lights gone black.

Coda

Her ease is your sloth, Catullus
you itch & roll in her ease:

former kings and cities
lost in the valley of her arm.

58

Lesbia, our Lesbia, the same old Lesbia,
Caelius, she whom Catullus loved once
more than himself and more than all his own,
loiters at the cross-roads

                     and in the backstreets
ready to toss-off the 'magnanimous' sons of Rome.

65

Although entangled in prolonged grief
severed from the company of the Muses
and far from Pieria
       my brain children still-born
myself among Stygian eddies
the eddies plucking at the pallid foot
of a brother
       who lies under Dardanian soil
stretched by the coastland
       whom none may now hear
none touch
       shuttered from sight
whom I treasured more than this life
and shall –
       in elegies of loss
plaintive as Procne crying under the shadow of the
   cypress
for lost Itylus,
       I send, Hortalus, mixed with misery
Berenice's Lock –
       clipped from Callimachus
for you might think my promise
had slipped like vague wind through my head
or was like the apple
       unavowed
the girl takes from her lover
       thrusts into her soft bodice

Catullus

and forgets there . . .
         till her mother takes her off guard –
she is startled,
        the love-fruit trundles ponderously across the
            floor
and the girl, blushing, stoops gingerly
                  to pick it up.

68

Borne down by bitter misfortune
you send me this letter, Manlius,
blotted with tears,
            it comes like flotsam
from a spumy sea –
            from the shipwreck of your affairs –
a cry from the undertow . . .
and that you,
            whom Venus deprives
of soft sleep,
            whom the Greek Muse
no longer tempts,
            who turn restlessly
in an empty bed,
            call me 'my friend',
that you look to Catullus
            for love-gifts of Venus
& of the Holy Muses,
            is a gift in itself,
but your own tears blind you to mine.
I am not neglectful of friendship,
but we two squat in the same coracle,
we are both swamped by the same stormy waters,
I have not the gifts of a happy man . . .
Often enough,
            when a man's toga first sat on my shoulders

I chased love & the Muses,
        in the onset of youth
the tart mixture of Venus
        seeming sweet,
but a brother's death
        drove a young man's kickshaws
into limbo –
        I have lost you, my brother
and your death has ended
        the spring season
of my happiness,
        our house is buried with you
& buried the laughter that you taught me.
There are no thoughts of love nor of poems
in my head
        since you died.
Hence, Manlius
        the reproach in your Roman letter
leaves me unmoved:
        'Why loiter in Verona,
Catullus, where
        for men of our circle
cold limbs in an empty bed
        are the rule –
not the exception?'
        Forgive me, my friend
but the dalliance of love
        that you look for
has been soured by mourning.
        As for a poem . . .

our tastes call for my Greek books,
          and those are at home
where we both live
          and where our years pile up,
in Rome . . .
          I have few copies of anything by me.
One case only has followed me North.
There is nothing curmudgeonly here –
on whom do you think
          I would sooner lavish
love-gifts of Venus
          & gifts of the Holy Muses
than you?
          You have turned to a friend
& the friend's hands are empty . . .
How can I give what I have not got?
                    [. . .]
               [Abridged.]

70

Lesbia says she'd rather marry me
than anyone,
      though Jupiter himself came asking
or so she says,
      but what a woman tells her lover in desire
should be written out on air & running water.

72

There was a time, Lesbia, when
you confessed only to Catullus in love:
you would set me above Jupiter himself.
I loved you then
        not as men love their women
but as a father his children – his family.
To-day I know you too well
        and desire burns deeper in me
and you are more coarse
        more frivolous in my thought.
'How,' you may ask, 'can this be?'
Such actions as yours excite
        increased violence of love,
Lesbia, but with friendless intention.

73

Cancel, Catullus, the expectancies of friendship
cancel the kindnesses deemed to accrue there:
kindness is barren, friendship breeds nothing,
only the weight of past deeds growing oppressive
as Catullus has discovered, bitter & troubled,
in one he had once accounted a unique friend.

75

Reason blinded by sin, Lesbia,
a mind drowned in its own devotion:
come clothed in your excellences –
I cannot think tenderly of you,
sink to what acts you dare –
I can never cut this love.

76

If evocations of past kindness shed
ease in the mind of one of rectitude,
of bond inviolate, who never in abuse of God
led men intentionally to harm,
such, as life lasts, must in Catullus shed
effect of joy from disregarded love.
For what by man can well in act or word
be done to others has by me been done
sunk in the credit of an unregarding heart.
Why protract this pain? why not resist
yourself in mind; from this point inclining
yourself back, breaking this fallen love
counter to what the gods desire of men?
Hard suddenly to lose love of long use,
hard precondition of your sanity
regained. Possible or not, this last
conquest is for you to make, Catullus.
May the pitying gods who bring
help to the needy at the point of death
look towards me and, if my life were clean,
tear this malign pest out from my body
where, a paralysis, it creeps from limb to limb
driving all former laughter from the heart.
I do not now expect – or want – my love returned,
nor cry to the moon for Lesbia to be chaste:
only that the gods cure me of this disease
and, as I once was whole, make me now whole again.

77

Whom I have trusted to no end (Rufus)
other than expense of evil knowledge
has come to the ambush,
        inflamed viscera,
raped all that was precious.
Here was poison in rape of life
        here was disease of love.
Witness the chaste mouth of a chaste woman
soiled by loathsome saliva –
        not with impunity:
your acts shall to succeeding ages
be by the bent Sibyl broadcast, in accents of infamy.

79

They nickname Lesbia's brother 'pulcher',
        naturally
since she prefers him to Catullus & the Catulli;
but let him dispose as he will of Catullus
        (& the Catulli)
when he finds three men of distinction
        willing to greet him in public.

83

Lesbia is extraordinarily vindictive
about me in front of her husband
who is thereby moved to fatuous laughter –
a man mulishly insensitive, failing to grasp
that a mindless silence (about me) spells safety
while to spit out my name in curses, baring
her white teeth, means she remembers me, and
what is more pungent still, is scratching the wound
ripening herself while she talks.

'*H*advantageous' breathes Arrius heavily
         when he means 'advantageous',
intending 'artificial' he labours '*h*artificial',
convinced he is speaking impeccably while
he blows his 'h's about most '*h*artificially'.
One understands that his mother – his uncle –
his family, in fact, on the distaff side
spoke so.

        Fortunately he was posted to Syria
and our ears grew accustomed to normal speech again,
unapprehensive for a while of such words
until suddenly the grotesque news reaches us
that the Ionian Sea has become
                since the advent of Arrius
no longer Ionian
        but (inevitably) *H*ionian.

85

I hate and I love. And if you ask me how,
I do not know: I only feel it, and I'm torn in two.

86

We have heard of Quintia's beauty. To me she is tall,
  slender
and of a white 'beauty'. Such things I freely admit;
but such things do not constitute beauty.
          In her there is nothing of Venus,
not a pinch of love spice in her long body.
While Lesbia, Lesbia is loveliness indeed.
          Herself of particular beauty
has she not plundered womanhead of all its graces,
          flaunting them as her adornment?

87

No woman loved, in truth, Lesbia
    as you by me;
no love-faith found so true
    as mine in you.

91

In this hopeless & wasting love of mine
I trusted you for one reason, Gellius:
not because I knew you well
        nor respected your constancy
nor thought you able (or willing) to rinse out your mind
but merely because the woman for whom
this compulsive desire is eating me
happens to be neither your mother
        nor sister
nor any other close female relative.
In spite of our intimacy I did not believe
you would find here incentive for action.
– You did,
        in the overwhelming attraction
pure sin holds for you, Gellius,
        or anything smacking of sin.

96

If, Calvus, effects of grief
           affect
those enigmatic sepulchres
           of former love
& spent friendships,
           lamented & evoked in our desire,
reflect, her early death
           will never grieve Quintilia
half so much
           as your long love must make her gay.

99

Purloining while you played in honeyed youth
a kiss, sweeter than one suspects ambrosia tastes,
I paid, Iuventius, in full:
                                    an hour or more
you racked me with my own self-exculpations
your loathing left untouched by tears.
No sooner had I kissed you
                                    than with every finger
in every corner of your mouth
                                    you washed & rubbed
all contact of my lips
                                    like the slaver of some syphilitic whore
away. More:
                    you gave me, fallen, to an enemy
                                                        – Amor
who has not since ceased to rack me in his own usage,
so that a purloined kiss
                                    once ambrosial,
is changed to one more acid than acid hellbane tastes.
Met with such strong despite of love
                                                my fallen love
shall from this day no kisses more purloin.

101

Journeying over many seas & through many countries
I come dear brother to this pitiful leave-taking
the last gestures by your graveside
the futility of words over your quiet ashes.
Life cleft us from each other
pointlessly depriving brother of brother.
Accept then, in our parents' custom
these offerings, this leave-taking
echoing for ever, brother, through a brother's tears.
                                   – 'Hail & Farewell'.

104

Do you really believe I could blacken my life,
the woman dearer to me than my two eyes?
If I could
        I should not be sunk in this way in my love for her –

who performs a zoo of two-backed beasts,
daily with Tappo.

107

If ever anyone anywhere, Lesbia, is looking
                    for what he knows will not happen
and then unexpectedly it happens –
                              the soul is astonished,
as we are now in each other,
                    an event dearer than gold,
for you have restored yourself, Lesbia, desired
restored yourself, longed for, unlooked for,
                              brought yourself back
to me. White day in the calendar!
                    Who happier than I?
What more can life offer
    than the longed for unlooked for event when it happens?

109

Joy of my life! you tell me this –
that nothing can possibly break this love of ours for each
    other.

God let her mean what she says,
                                from a candid heart,
that our two lives may be linked in their length
day to day,
        each to each,
in a bond of sacred fidelity.